TEAMWORK

Quotations to inspire and celebrate our team.

Compiled by Dan Zadra
Designed by Kobi Yamada
and Steve Potter

COM·PEN·DI·UM™
Publishing

LYNNWOOD, WASHINGTON

ACKNOWLEDGEMENTS
These quotations were gathered lovingly but unscientifically over several years and/or contributed by many friends or acquaintances. Some arrived, and survived in our files, on scraps of paper and may therefore be imperfectly worded or attributed. To the authors, contributors and original sources, our thanks, and where appropriate, our apologies.
—The editors

CREDITS
Compiled by Dan Zadra
Designed by Kobi Yamada and Steve Potter

ISBN 1-888387-97-1

Printed in China

TEAMWORK

A Gift to Inspire and Celebrate Your Achievements

*Success is always sweetest
when it's shared.*
—Howard Schultz

It's a competitive world out there, and it's accelerating. One person can still do something, but one person can't do everything.

The greatest success stories of today are being created, not necessarily by the most talented people, but by the most cohesive teams. John Wooden put it this way: "If you want to win, don't play your eleven best—play your best eleven." Dr. Rob Gilbert put it this way: "The best team doesn't win nearly as often as the team that gets along best." All true.

Great companies know this secret, have always known it: Whenever you can hook the right dream to the right team, all the old limitations go out the window. Suddenly, anything becomes possible, and nothing is too good to be true.

What makes a great team? The book-shelves are filled with complex answers and complicated theories. But the following pages are alive with inspiring reminders that it's really the "little things" that make a good team great: Help each other be right, not wrong. Look for ways to make new ideas work, not for reasons they won't. Pit yourselves against the goal, not each other. Do everything with enthusiasm, it's contagious. And, as Starbuck's Howard Schultz reminds us: "Try to reach the finish line together. Success is always sweetest when it's shared."

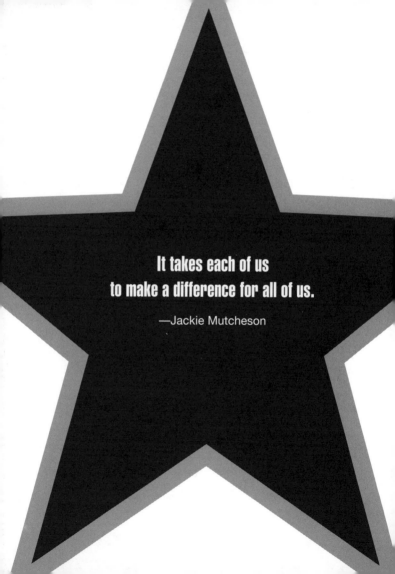

It takes each of us
to make a difference for all of us.

—Jackie Mutcheson

The world is before us
and we need not take it or
leave it as it was when
we came in.

JAMES BALDWIN

It isn't where
we came from; it's where
we're going that counts.

ELLA FITZGERALD

We define ourselves
by the best that is in us,
not the worst that
has been done to us.

EDWARD LEWIS

We cannot become
what we want to be by
remaining what we are.

MAX DEPREE

A single idea
can transform a life,
a team, a business,
a nation, a world.

ANON

Anything can happen
with the right team.
That's the beauty of creating.

ERNIE HARWELL

It's not who we are
that holds us back, it's
who we think we're not.

MICHAEL NOLAN

When we're
through changing,
we're through.

BRUCE BARTON

Yesterday's answer
has nothing to do with
today's problem.

BILL GATES, MICROSOFT

Change is inevitable.
It's direction that counts.

GIL ATKINSON

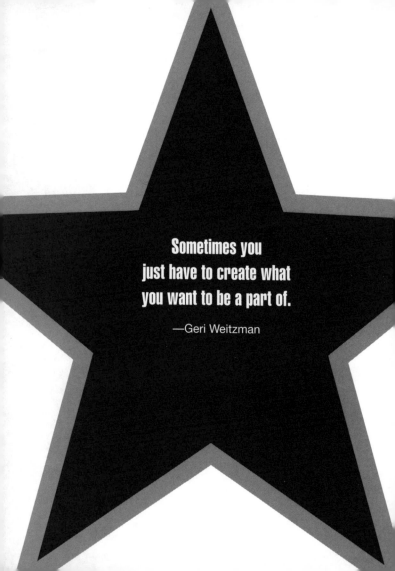

**Sometimes you
just have to create what
you want to be a part of.**

—Geri Weitzman

The future cannot
be predicted, but futures
can be invented. It is our
ability to invent the future
which gives us hope and
makes us what we are.

DENNIS GABOR

Everything that is
was once imagined.

TED JONES

At times it is necessary
to go over the top. How else
can we get to the other side?

KOBI YAMADA

We aren't forced to follow
the old ideas.

J. GEORGE BENDORZ

New ideas...
are not born in a
conforming environment.

ROGER VON OECH

Don't expect anything
original from an echo.

DUNC MUNCY

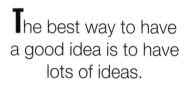

The best way to have
a good idea is to have
lots of ideas.

DR. LINUS PAULING

Thousands of perceptions
race through our brains
every day. Some seem crazy
but are pure genius. Give them
the red light for at least long
enough to write them down.

RALPH M. FORD

Excellent organizations
and teams are
experimenters supreme.

TOM PETERS

★

Little people keep secrets.
Big people share ideas.

PHIL ROGNIER

Blessed are the curious
for they shall have adventures.

LOVELLE DRACHMAN

Discoveries are often made
by not following instructions,
by going off the main road,
by trying the untried.

FRANK TYGER

The brain is a mass
cranial nerve tissue, most
of it in mint condition.

ROBERT HALF

Some people get lost in
thought because it's such
unfamiliar territory.

G. BEHN

Creativity is inventing,
experimenting, growing,
taking risks, breaking rules,
making mistakes,
and having fun.

MARY LOU COOK

★

You have a creative
contribution to make.
Our lives will be better
if you do.

MICHAEL TOMS

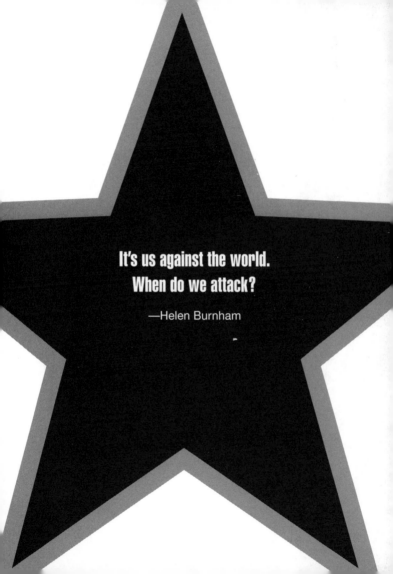

It's us against the world.
When do we attack?

—Helen Burnham

Why be afraid
of something we want?

MOSLEY

We see something
that has to be done
and we organize it.

ELINOR GUGGENHEIMER

There is somebody
smarter than any of us,
and that is all of us.

MICHAEL NOLAN

Focused action beats
brilliance any day.

ART TUROCK

We don't grow
unless we take risks.
Any successful company or
team is riddled with failures.

JAMES E. BURKE

It is the business of
the future to be dangerous.

ALFRED NORTH WHITEHEAD

You can do
anything in this world if
you are prepared to take
the consequences.

W. SOMERSET MAUGHAM

Go in over your head,
not just up to your neck.

DOROTHEA LANG

7/29/08

Everyone in a successful organization must be willing to risk. Risk is like change; it's not a choice.

MAX DEPREE

The freedom to fail is vital to success.

MICHAEL KORDA

Unless commitment
is made, there are only
promises and hopes;
but no plans.

PETER DRUCKER

The first step towards getting
somewhere is to decide
that you are not going
to stay where you are.

2/12/8

J. PIERPONT MORGAN

3/24/09

So what do we do?
Anything. Something.
So long as we just don't sit
there. If we screw it up,
start over. Try something else.
If we wait until we've satisfied
all the uncertainties,
it may be too late.

LEE IACOCCA

All of us can take steps—
no matter how small and
insignificant at the start—
in the direction we want to go.

MARSHA SINETAR

It's the start that
stops most people.

BOB ROGNIER

We're going to
stop procrastinating,
just you wait and see.

GRAFFITO

What isn't tried
won't work.

BERNIE SIEGEL

Nothing will ever be
attempted, if all possible
objections must first
be overcome.

SAMUEL JOHNSON

The only real
menace is inertia.

ST. JOHN PERSE

We never know
how good we are,
until we are called to rise.

EMILY DICKINSON

Do something.
If it doesn't work,
do something else.
Nothing is too crazy.

JIM HIGHTOWER

Do-so is more
important than say-so.

PETE SEEGER

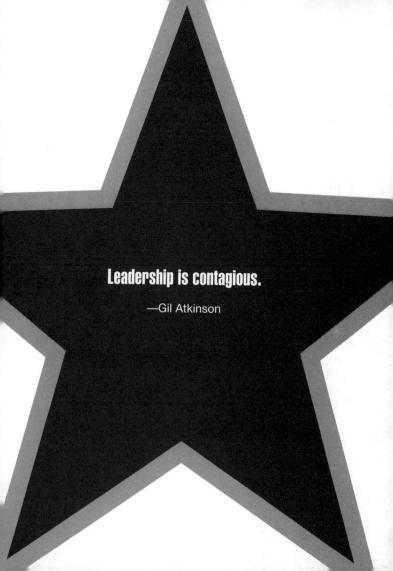

Leadership is contagious.

—Gil Atkinson

On the best teams
everyone leads.

FAYE LAPOINTE

If you tell people
the destination, but not
how to get there, you'll be
amazed at the results.

GEORGE PATTON

I don't believe in
ordering people to do things.
You have to sort of grab
an oar and row with them.

HAROLD GENEEN

The best leaders will be
those who listen to their
people to figure out where
they should be going.

JACK KAHL

Those who enjoy responsibility usually get it; those who merely like excercising authority usually lose it.

MALCOLM FORBES

My experience has taught me that whatever we have to do usually can be done.

CATHY CAPPETTA

Impossible is
just an opinion.

GIL ATKINSON

Specialize in doing
what you can't.

HENRIETTA MEARS

I cannot discover
anyone who knows
enough to say what is
and what is not possible.

HENRY FORD

I am looking for a lot
of people who have an
infinite capacity to not
know what can't be done.

HENRY FORD

No opportunity
should be avoided
merely because it is
impossible.

RICHARD R. GREEN

Champions are their own
experts. They want to know,
"Who says so?"

ROB GILBERT

We can if we will.

—Frank Vizzare

Life's under
no obligation to give us
what we expect.

MARGARET MITCHELL

Life is what we make it,
always has been,
always will be.

GRANDMA MOSES

41

There will be those
who will tell us we can't
make it because we're too
small, because we're too
inexperienced, because of
how we look, or how we talk.
We all have heard that…
I almost listened.

L. DOUGLAS WILDER

We have seen
too much pessimism, too
much of a negative approach.
The answer is simple; if we
want something very badly,
we can achieve it.

MARGO JONES

When everyone is
against you, it means that
you are absolutely wrong—
or absolutely right.

ALBERT GUINON

Remember, there is
no problem so big that we
can't handle it together.

SOPHIE YOUNG

You win some
and you learn some.

BARRY JOHNSON

Champions keep playing
until they get it right.

BILLIE JEAN KING

At the end of every hard day, people still find some reason to believe.

BRUCE SPRINGSTEEN

Foster the attitude, "let's fix the problem, not place the blame."

BUILDING COMMUNITY

If you are committed
to creating value, and if
you aren't afraid of the hard
times, obstacles become
utterly unimportant.

CANDICE CARPENTER

It ain't as bad as
you think. It will look
better in the morning.

COLIN POWELL

Most of the important things in the world have been accomplished by people who have kept on trying when there seemed to be no hope at all.

DALE CARNEGIE

Perseverance and audacity generally win.

DORTHEE DELUZY

There is nothing we cannot live down, rise above and overcome.

ELLA WHEELER-WILCOX

We are not retreating—we are advancing in another direction.

GENERAL DOUGLAS MACARTHUR

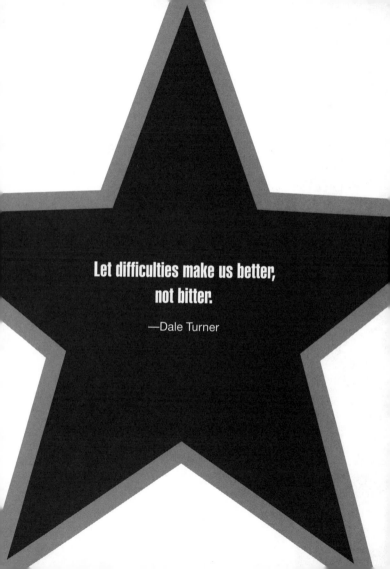

Let difficulties make us better,
not bitter.

—Dale Turner

The minute you start
talking about what you're
going to do if you lose,
you have lost.

GEORGE SCHULTZ

I always tried to turn
every disaster into
an opportunity.

JOHN D. ROCKEFELLER

Each problem has
a hidden opportunity so
powerful that it literally dwarfs
the problem. The greatest
success stories were created
by people who recognized
a problem and turned
it into an opportunity.

JOSEPH SUGARMAN

To swear off making mistakes
is very easy. All you have to do
is swear off having ideas.

LEO BURNETT

If you have a job
without aggravations,
you don't have a job.

MALCOLM FORBES

In the game of life
nothing is less important
than the score at half time.

UNKNOWN

The first time you quit,
it's hard. The second time
it gets easier. The third time,
you don't even have to
think about it.

PAUL "BEAR" BRYANT

Consider every mistake
you do as an asset.

PAUL J. MEYER

Problems can become opportunities when the right people come together.

ROBERT REDFORD

All of us must learn this lesson somewhere— that it costs something to be what we are.

SHIRLEY ABBOTT

Let the ideas clash but not the hearts.

—C.C. Mehta

Success without conflict is unrealistic.

ROBERT SCHULLER

Great teams set aside personal agendas to focus all their resources on a common goal.

AL SCHMITT

No one wants advice,
we want collaboration.

RIAN JONES

Why is there no
conflict at this meeting?
Something's wrong when
there's no conflict.

MICHAEL EISNER

When two people
always agree, one of them
is unnecessary.

WILLIAM WRIGLEY, JR.

You don't get harmony
when everybody sings
the same note.

DOUG FLOYD

If everyone is thinking alike, someone isn't thinking.

GENERAL GEORGE PATTON

Where you want the contest is not among people, but among ideas.

CASEY COWELL

Pit yourself
against the goal
rather than each other.

DAN ZADRA

All life is a negotiation.

WENDY WASSERSTEIN

Blessed are the flexible
for they shall not be bent
out of shape.

DON WARD

Nothing produces such
odd results as trying
to get even.

FRANKLIN P. JONES

We can't move ahead
if we're trying to get even!

FRANK TYGER

Get mad.
Then get over it.

COLIN POWELL

When we criticize, we
separate ourselves from
the solution. We've got
to jump right in there
with both feet.

DOLORES HUERTA

Comunication loves
a vacuum.

DAN ZADRA

If you don't give people information, they'll make up something to fill the void.

CARLA O'DELL

★

They'll tell you, 'Quit now, you'll never make it.' If you disregard that advice, you'll be halfway there.

DAVID ZUCKER

It's easy to play a joke
on people who like to argue.
Agree with them.

TED HOWE

The one who strikes first
admits that his or her ideas
have given out.

DON WARD

If you never budge,
don't expect a push.

MALCOLM FORBES

If you can't add
to the discussion,
don't subtract from it.

DENNIS CRIMP

Trust is a treasured item.

DON WARD

Trust each other again
and again. When the trust
level gets high enough,
people transcend apparent
limits, discovering new and
awesome abilities for which
they were previously unaware.

DAVID ARMISTEAD

Let's go the extra mile.
It's never crowded.

—Dennis Crimp

Open your arms to change,
but don't let go of your values.

DON WARD

What people say
is important, what they do
is more important, but what
they value is most important.

BUILDING COMMUNITY

If we lose our
core values, we
lose ourselves.

HENRY MCCOY

Be a yardstick of quality.
Some people aren't used
to an environment where
excellence is expected.

STEVEN JOBS

Quality is not only right, it's free. And it is not only free, it is the most profitable product line we have.

HAROLD GENEEN

Quality is not any single thing but an aura, an atmosphere, an over-powering feeling that your team is doing everything with excellence.

JACK WELCH

Beautiful things
make money.

GEOFFREY BEENE

We knew we loved making
cookies and every time we did,
we made people happy.
That was our business plan.

DEBBI FIELDS

Giving people a little more
than they expect is a good
way to get back a lot more
than you'd expect.

ROBERT HALF

How come everybody wants
to be on a championship team,
but nobody wants
to come to practice?

BOBBY KNIGHT

We're gonna get in
two good hours of practice
even if it takes six hours.

LOU HOLTZ, COLLEGE FOOTBALL COACH

If you have always
done it that way, it is
probably wrong.

CHARLES KETTERING

Our checks that
go to our people say,
'From our customers,'
because we want to remind
ourselves that it's not some
addition to the general office
that produces that check;
it's our customers.

HERB KELLEHER, SOUTHWEST AIRLINES

We all need to believe
in what we are doing.

ALLAN D. GILMOUR

People don't just
go to work to acquire,
they go to become.

DAN ZADRA

Making a living
is only part of life.

CECIL ANDRUS

It's a great satisfaction knowing that for a brief point in time you made a difference.

IRENE NATIVIDAD

Living is more a question of what one spends than what one makes.

MARCEL DUCHAMP

Draw strength from each other.

—James A. Renier

What have you done
for your team TODAY?

WILLIAM PLATT

Let's all strategize how the
job can get done versus
informing each other why
it can't be done.

MELISSA GONSALES

We can always depend
on some people to make the
best, instead of the worst,
of whatever happens.

SANDRA WILDE

If you look for the good
in others, you'll discover
the best in yourself!

BOB MOAWAD

It's not the critic who counts.

THEODORE ROOSEVELT

Help each other be right,
not wrong. Look for ways
to make new ideas work,
not for reasons they won't.
Do everything with enthusiasm,
it's contagious.

IAN PERCY

It is easier to pull down
than to build up.

FRANK VIZZARE

Look, when that crowd gets
to cheering, when we know
they're with us, when we know
they like us, we play better.
A hell of a lot better!

BILL CARLIN

12/4/07

It all boils down to
two questions: Are we
operating with excitement and
passion? Do we respect
and support each other?
If so, we're going to excel.

GEORGE SCHULTZ

Is not life a
hundred times too short
for us to bore ourselves?

FRIEDRICH NIETZSCHE

Act like you expect
to get into the end zone.

JOE PATERNO

Any fool can criticize,
condemn and complain—
and most do.

DALE CARNEGIE

Give me the benefit of
your convictions, if you
have any; but keep your
doubts to yourself, for I have
enough of my own.

JOHANN WOLFGANG VON GOETHE

Let's be sensitive to the
things people have been
through. We are all bruised.

WILL KIEM

How long does it take
to stop, smile and lift
someone's spirits?
Just a tiny little minute—
but Eternity is in it.

KEYNOTE

Your luck is how
you treat people.

BRIDGET O'DONNELL

Be as hard as the world
requires you to be, and
as soft as the world
allows you to be.

JAPANESE SAYING

It may be in fact utterly
impossible to be successful
without helping others to
become successful.

MAYA ANGELOU

There is no "them and us." In a world this size there can only be "we"—all of us working together.

DON WARD

If you don't realize there is always somebody who knows how to do something better than you, then you don't give proper respect for others' talents.

HORTENSE CANADY

To put yourself in
another's place requires
real imagination.

JULIETTE LOW

7/21/09

Diversity is a competitive
advantage. Different people
approach similar problems
in different ways.

RICH MCGINN

It's the things
in common that make
relationships enjoyable, but
it's the little differences that
make them interesting.

TODD RUTHMAN

Seeking diversity
automatically leads us to
excellence, just as focusing
on excellence inevitably
leads us to diversity.

WILLIAM C. STEERE

Let's celebrate the
differences.

JAMES WILL

We are all unique, and
if that is not fulfilled, then
something wonderful
has been lost.

MARTHA GRAHAM

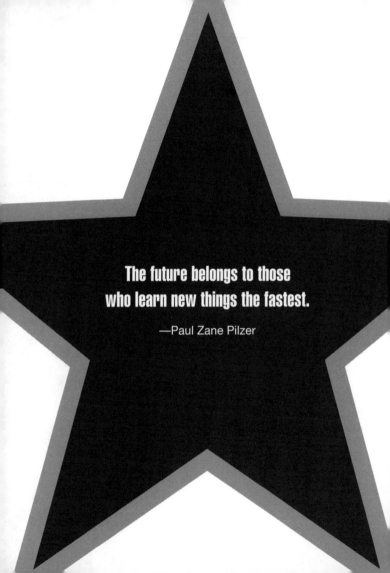

The future belongs to those
who learn new things the fastest.

—Paul Zane Pilzer

School is always
in session.

PHILIP ALLEN

Learning is not compulsory,
but neither is survival.

W. EDWARDS DEMING

In our rapidly changing world, it's not our "know-how," but our "learn-how" that will ensure our success.

LARRY WILSON

Each of us has special talents. It's our duty to make the most of them.

ROBERT E. ALLEN

It's what we learn
after we know it all
that counts.

JOHN WOODEN

If we don't change,
we don't grow. If we
don't grow, we are
not really living.

GAIL SHEEHY

Whatever has
crowded out growth
needs to be recognized
and removed.

JEAN SHINODA BOLEN

Education is hanging around
until you've caught on.

ROBERT FROST

The difference
between great and average
or lousy in any job is, mostly,
having the imagination and
desire to re-create
yourself daily.

TOM PETERS

The trouble with organizing
a thing is that pretty soon folks
get to paying more attention
to the organization than to
what they're organizing for.

LAURA INGALLS WILDER

A committee takes
hours to put into minutes
what can be done in seconds.

JUDY CASTRINA

We will be remembered
for all the rules we break.

DOUGLAS MACARTHUR

Rules? What rules?
We're trying to
accomplish something!

THOMAS EDISON

Getting into trouble
is our genius and glory.

JOHN PFEIFFER

Few will have the greatness to bend history itself; but each of us can work to change a small portion of events, and in the total of all those acts will be written the history of this generation.

ROBERT F. KENNEDY

Goodwill is the mightiest practical force in the universe.

C.F. DOLE

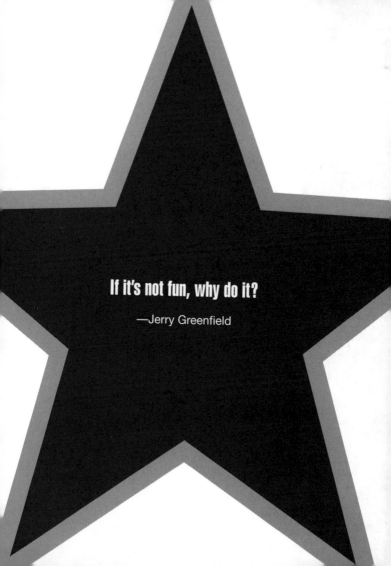

If it's not fun, why do it?

—Jerry Greenfield

People are always good company when they are doing what they really enjoy.

SAMUEL BUTLER

As usual, the serious me is working hard, but the real me is having fun.

JOHN REED

Serious people have
few ideas. People with
ideas are never serious.

PAUL VALERY

People come together
because they need each
other and they need to hear
victories about each other.

BILL MILLIKEN

TEAMWORK

When someone
does something good,
applaud! You will make
two people happy.

SAMUEL GOLDWYN

The deepest priciple in
human nature is the
craving to be appreciated.

WILLIAM JAMES

The five most
important words:
"You did a great job."

UNKNOWN

Celebrate whenever you can,
'cause this is it folks, it's not
a dress rehearsal.

ANITA RODDICK

Failures are few
among people who have
found a work they enjoy
enough to do it well.
You invest time in your work;
invest love in it too.

CLARENCE FLYNN

★

If everyone
is moving forward
together, then success
will take care of itself.

HENRY FORD

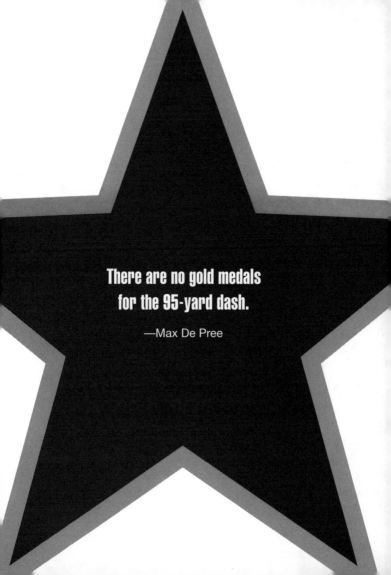

There are no gold medals
for the 95-yard dash.

—Max De Pree

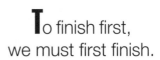

To finish first,
we must first finish.

RICK MEARS

There are no
shortcuts to any place
worth going.

BEVERLY SILLS

Anybody can quit.
It's exactly·what your
adversaries or competitors
hope you will do.

DAN ZADRA

Others can stop you
temporarily. Only you
can do it permanently.

KEYNOTE

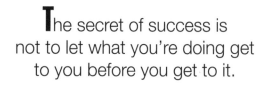

The secret of success is
not to let what you're doing get
to you before you get to it.

KOBI YAMADA

★

Life's real tragedy is when
we do not realize how close
we were to success when
we gave up.

ANON

The greatest thing
is to fight life through,
and say at the end,
"The dream is true."

EDWIN MARKHAM

We are very near to greatness:
one step and we are safe;
can we not take the leap?
We can!

—**EMERSON**

STAR ★ SERIES

Also available from
Compendium Publishing
are these spirited companion
books in the Star Series
of great quotations:

GOALS

LEADERSHIP

MOTIVATION

These books may be ordered directly
from the publisher (800) 914-3327.
But please try your local bookstore first!

www.compendiuminc.com